www.inkytreasure.com
Learn. Play. Educate.

BIRDS
COLOUR BY NUMBER

This book belongs to

SPARROW

1=Sky Blue   2=Ice Blue   3=Dark Brown   4=Yellow

5=Dark Grey   6=Red   7=Light Grey

OWL

| 1=Dark Blue | 2=Dark Brown | 3=Brown | 4=Light Brown |
| 5=Light Grey | 6=Yellow | 7=Grey | 8=Black |

CRANE

1=Sky Blue   2=Red   3=Dark Brown   4=Light Brown

5=Grey   6=Dark Grey   7=Light Blue   8=Black

QUAIL

1=Sky Blue   2=Ice Blue   3=Dark Brown   4=Light Brown

5=Dark Grey   6=Dark Blue   7=Yellow   8=Green

PIGEON

1=Sky Blue   2=Ice Blue   3=Grey   4=Dark Grey

5=Dark Grey   6= Black

PARROT

1=Ice Blue	2=Grey	3=Dark Brown	4=Dark Grey
5= Pink	6=Green	7= Light Green	8= Red

SWAN

1=Sky Blue   2=Ice Blue   3=Light Blue   4=Grey

5= Dark Grey   6=Orange   7= Green

OSTRICH

1=Sky Blue   2=Yellow   3=Pink   4=Grey

5=Black   6=Dark Grey   7= Green   8=Light Brown

KINGFISHER

1=Sky Blue   2=Blue   3=Light Orange   4=Light Brown
5=Light Blue   6=Green   7=Red   8=Dark Brown

PEACOCK

1=Sky Blue　　　2=Ice Blue　　　3=Navy Blue　　　4=Green

5=Light Brown　　6=Dark Grey　　7=Light Yellow　　8=Light Blue

WOODPECKER

1=Sky Blue   2=Black   3=Light Orange   4=Red

5=Grey   6=Green   7=Dark Grey   8=Dark Brown

SWALLOW

1=Sky Blue   2=Ice Blue   3=Dark Blue   4=Red

5=Yellow   6=Green

DUCK

1=Sky Blue   2=Light Blue   3=Orange   4=Yellow

5=Green

PENGUIN

1=Sky Blue   2=Ice Blue   3=Orange   4=Light Blue

5=Black   6=Grey   7= DarkGrey

FLAMINGO

1=Sky Blue   2=Purple   3=Light Pink   4=Dark Pink

5=Black   6=Dark Grey   7= Green   8=Light Brown

HEN

1=Sky Blue   2=Light Brown   3=Red   4=Dark Red

5=Grey   6=Dark Grey   7= Green   8= Drak Brown

TOUCAN

1=Sky Blue   2=Light Brown   3=Orange   4=Red

5=Black   6=Grey   7= Green   8=Dark grey

VULTURE

1=Sky Blue   2=Green   3=Dark Brown   4=Brown

5=Yellow   6=Pink   7=Grey

EAGLE

1=Sky Blue   2=Green   3=Dark Brown   4=Brown

5=Yellow   6=Light Brown

CROW

1=Sky Blue   2=Ice Blue   3=Dark Brown   4=Light Brown

5= Light Grey   6=Dark Grey   7= Green   8= Yellow

Do you like the book? Please share your feedback?

Thank you
Sachin Sachdeva (Author & Illustrator)
www.inkytreasure.com

You can give your feedback and suggestions on Amazon.com

Printed in Great Britain
by Amazon